THE SIGN OF JONAH

The
Universal Publishing
A s s o c i a t i o n

TRACT NO. 10

Revised Edition

The Universal Publishing Association

P.O. Box 24027

Waco, Texas 76702

UniversalPublishing.com

ISBN: 978-1-962573-16-0

PRINTED IN U.S.A.

"The Sign of Jonah"

AND

QUESTION AND ANSWER DISCUSSION

MATT. 12:39, 40

Though a number of times we have conclusively cleared the questions as to (1) whether Jesus, in order to fulfill the "sign of Jonah," was "three days and three nights" in the grave, or (2) whether the sign was fulfilled in some other way, and (3) whether He was crucified on Friday, on Thursday, or on Wednesday, there still seem to be some points which are not clear to all, first of which underlies the question:

> *Was Christ Crucified on the Day the*
> *Leaven Was Put Out of the Houses—*
> *On the Fourteenth Day?*

Mark, who was an eyewitness of the event, says, "And the first day of unleavened bread, *when they killed* the passover, His disciples said unto Him, Where wilt Thou that we go and prepare that Thou mayest eat the passover? And He sendeth forth two of His disciples, and saith unto them, Go ye into the city, and there shall meet you a man bearing a pitcher of water: follow him. . . . And His disciples went forth, and came into the city, and found as He had said unto them: and they made ready the passover. And in the evening *He cometh with* the *twelve*. And as they sat and *did eat*, Jesus said, Verily I say unto you, One of you which eateth with Me shall betray Me." Mark 14:12, 13, 16-18.

Since the Passover lamb was killed in the evening of the fourteenth day of the first month (Ex. 12:6), and was eaten at the commencement of the fifteenth day (Num. 28:17), and since the gospel writers declare that Jesus ate the Passover at the very hour the whole Jewish nation ate it, the fact is solidly established that the time of the crucifixion of Christ did not coincide with the time of the killing of the lamb on the fourteenth day for the first of the Passover feasts. It did coincide, however, with the killing of the lamb for the second of the feasts, as will be seen from the following paragraphs.

Even astronomical records agree that the fourteenth-day sacrifice of the Passover supper that year came on Wednesday, and the Bible emphatically states that the feast of the Passover was to be observed on the fifteenth day (Num. 28:17), Thursday that year. Jesus, therefore, could not have been crucified on either of these two days. This is borne out by the fact that, as stated before, He observed the first of the feasts with the disciples. Moreover, Matthew 26:5 plainly states that the assembly of the priests and the scribes, with Caiaphas in the judgment seat, decided not to kill Him "on the feast day"—Thursday, the fifteenth. Hence the question: Why does the Bible say He was crucified on

The Preparation Day?

Mark's statement, "The preparation, that is, the day before the Sabbath" (Mark 15:42), explains that this preparation day was Friday, "the day before the Sabbath." And as this same Sabbath, John calls "an high day" (John 19:31), it could only have been the seventh-day Sabbath in the Passover week, a sabbath within a Sabbath, for the Passover week was a seven-day occasion (Num. 28:17), and therefore in each week of Passover there was a seventh-day Sabbath, and hence two holy days in one day—an high day.

Although in the Scriptures a group of feast days are sometimes called sabbath days, or sabbaths, the Passover in itself is never called *the* Sabbath. This is especially true throughout the New Testament. And for any of the apostles to call the Passover day, *the* Sabbath day, is for them not only to ignore reason, but also to confuse *the* Passover with the "seventh-day Sabbath," the only day ever called "the Sabbath."

Thus from this angle also it is made clear that the "preparation" day, the day they crucified Jesus, was Friday—the preparation for the Sabbath in the Passover week; that the Passover lamb, which was killed on Wednesday (the fourteenth day), did not coincide with the crucifixion; and that Jesus ate the Passover on Thursday (the fifteenth day), was arrested the same day before daybreak, crucified on Friday (the sixteenth), buried before the Sabbath, and resurrected on Sunday (the eighteenth). These Biblical facts, which are supported also by tradition, give rise to the question:

Was Not Jesus Three Days and Three Nights in the Tomb?

Let it not be forgotten that He was buried on the day called the "preparation day," Friday, and that the chief priests and the Pharisees went to Pilate on the "day that followed the day of the preparation" (Matt. 27:62), on Sabbath, requesting him to set a watch over the tomb. It was therefore the second night after His burial that the tomb was guarded. And the fact that this was the night that Jesus arose (Matt. 28:1-5), proves that He was in the tomb only the two nights— Friday night and Saturday night. Consequently the statement, "three days and three nights in *the heart* of the earth," must stand for something more than simply His being in the grave, as interpreted by some.

Then in Matthew 28:1, the words, "as it began to dawn toward the first day of the week," are not spoken with intention to tell the time when Jesus arose, but to show the time when the women arrived at the tomb, and therefore cannot be taken to mean, as some think, the evening at the end of the Sabbath. For the women came to the sepulchre in the morning, as each gospel writer attests:

Luke—   "Now upon the first day of the week, very early in the morning, they came unto the sepulchre." Luke 24:1.

Mark—   "And very early in the morning the first day of the week, they came unto the sepulchre at the rising of the sun." Mark 16:2.

John—   "The first day of the week cometh Mary Magdalene early, when it was yet dark, unto the sepulchre." John 20:1.

Matthew— "In the end of the Sabbath, as it began to dawn toward the first day of the week [not as it began to turn toward the first *night* of the week], came Mary Magdalene and the other Mary to see the sepulchre." Matt. 28:1.

The statement that Mary Magdalene and the other Mary came to see the sepulchre "as it began to *dawn* toward the first day of the week" (Matt. 28:1), has been interpreted by some to mean that they came to the sepulchre on the Sabbath, before sunset, and then found that the Lord had already risen. But let it be remembered that on the day when they came, Mary met the Lord Himself and talked with Him. If, therefore, she was told on the Sabbath by the angels that Jesus had risen from the dead, and she herself then saw the sepulchre empty, also talked with the Lord (Matt. 28:1-9), why should she play the fool on Sunday morning by going to the sepulchre to see the Lord's body, as though she knew nothing about His resurrection, when instead she should have heeded His instructions to give the news to the disciples, and to meet Him in Galilee (Matt. 28:1-7; John 20:1-17)?

Mark 16:1, 2 and Luke 24:1-10, also John 20:1, bear threefold proof that in regard to the Lord's resurrection, Mary Magdalene knew nothing before Sunday morning, when to her surprise the angel said: "He is risen; He is not here: behold the place where they laid Him. But go your way, tell His disciples and Peter that He goeth before you into Galilee: there shall ye see Him." Mark 16:6, 7.

Then, too, Mark says that "Jesus was risen early the first day of the week," and also that on "the first day of the week [not on the Sabbath], He appeared first to Mary Magdalene." Mark 16:9.

Those, therefore, who interpret the

words, "as it began to dawn toward the first day of the week," to mean that it was late Sabbath afternoon, and that Jesus was then risen, are in serious error.

Mark says, "*when the Sabbath was past*," whereas Matthew says, "*in the end of the Sabbath*." In another instance, the one says, "*very early in the morning* the first day of the week"; whereas the other says, "*as it began to dawn toward* the first day of the week." These comparative phrases all have the same significance.

And furthermore, a comparison of Matthew 28:1 and John 20:1 shows that both scriptures refer to one and the same event, though many try to refute the fact. John says that the women came to the sepulchre "the first day of the week . . . when it was *yet* dark." This cannot mean in the end of the Sabbath as the sun was about to set, for had that been the time, John would not have said, "when it was *yet* dark," plainly indicating that the night had almost worn away, but not completely. And Matthew, speaking of this same time, says: "in the end of the Sabbath, as it began to *dawn* toward the first day of the week."

Thus in the light of all the gospels, the word "dawn" can be interpreted to mean only the breaking of day—the morning. The English dictionary also supports this definition.

Now, even a cursory analysis of these four synoptic passages can result in but the one conclusion that all four observers are writing of the same event (the visit of Mary Magdalene and the other Mary to the tomb), of the same place (Christ's sepulchre), and of the same time (early in the morning, the first day of the week), only each stating the matter in his own words—a threefold conclusion which is further borne out by examining the subject from the angle of

The Hour of Each Event.

Anciently, the timepiece was regulated at twelve, sunset. Midnight and noon were at the sixth hour, and morning at the twelfth hour. From this original system of timekeeping, the record in connection with the trial and with the crucifixion is made as follows:

John's record of the trial states that Jesus was in Pilate's judgment hall at "about the sixth hour" (John 19:14), whereas Mark's record of the crucifixion states that Jesus was hanging on the cross at "the sixth hour." Mark 15:33. Obviously, these two "sixth" hours cannot be the same, for at the first sixth hour He was on trial in Pilate's judgment hall, whereas at the next "sixth hour" (three hours after He was crucified, and while He was hanging on the cross) the sun became darkened: after three more hours, —from "the sixth hour" to "the ninth hour," when the sun again appeared (Mark 15:33),—Jesus died (Mark 15:37).

But there being still another private opinion on this point, we shall analyze a resultant question,

Was Not the Time Then Designated
by "Watches"?

To attempt to construe the hours on record as "watches"—periods of four hours—rather than as actual hours of day and night, is to strain reason to a breaking point in the interest of the idea that all in connection with the Passover, the trial, and the crucifixion took place in one day!

As far as we know, all Bible students agree that Jesus was crucified during the day and was buried before sunset. And as only the hours of the night were ever reckoned by "watches," the "watch" periods are foolishly dragged into the discussion. So being wholly irrelevant in this connection, they by all rights merit no consideration. For the sake, however, of those who really want the truth, but who are confused over the idea under discussion, we shall give it brief treatment.

As the "watch" theory cannot be imposed upon the hours during the day, we have no choice but to conclude that Jesus was crucified at the actual third hour (Mark 15:25); that three hours later the sun was darkened at the actual sixth hour (Mark 15:33); and that after three more hours, Jesus died and the sun again appeared at the actual ninth hour of the day (Mark 15:34-37), and not at a certain "watch" of the night.

And as there are not two sixth hours but only one sixth hour in a day, therefore the sixth hour at the time of the trial in Pilate's judgment hall, and the sixth hour at the time of the darkening of the sun, which came three hours after Jesus was nailed to the cross, are not four hours apart, but either twelve or twenty-four hours apart! Manifestly, therefore, even though one resort to the device of the "watch" system, one cannot rationally conclude that the trial and the darkening of the sun, not to mention the events connected with them, came the same day. Necessarily they took longer.

Then, too, as there are twelve hours, or four "watches," between this particular trial and the darkening of the sun, and as He was crucified at the third hour (nine hours after the trial, and three hours before the time that the sun was darkened), it is folly to try to crowd this actual twelve-hour period into a four-hour "watch"; and still worse folly is it to try to do so if the trial were at Thursday noon.

The gospel writers do not mean "watches" when they say "hours," for Jesus did not teach them to say, There are four watches in the day; but rather, There are twelve hours in the day (John 11:9). Moreover, as aforestated, never the day, but only the night, was divided into watches. And, furthermore, the clock dials were never marked by watches, but by hours, and when they said "hours," they never meant "watches." These evidences wholly discredit the "watch" scheme of interpretation.

Hold not to what fabricated ideas seem to make the Scriptures say, but grip tenaciously to what the Word, in simplicity, plainly says. Following this procedure, let us now review this study in the ensuing

Summary.

The Hours of the Night

(Sunset) 1-2-3-4-5-6-7-8-9-10-11-12

The Hours of the Day

(Sunrise) 1-2-3-4-5-6-7-8-9-10-11-12

By checking, on the diagram above, the hours mentioned by the gospel writers, the reader will see that there is no possible way by which to make all these events occupy one day only. To begin with, check the first "sixth hour"—the trial (John 19:14); then check the "third hour"—the crucifixion, (Mark 15:25); next, check the second "sixth hour"—the darkening of the sun (Mark 15:33); then, the "ninth hour"

—the death (Mark 15:34-38); and last, the "twelfth hour"—the burial (Mark 15:42, 46).

From this it will be seen that all these events did not take place in one twelve-hour day, and that necessarily, therefore, Christ was brought before Pilate either at midnight preceding Friday morning or at noon Thursday. To determine which, we need only consult John's record of the trial, which disallows the midday time of Thursday, for it says: "It was the preparation of the passover." John 19:14. And as this "preparation" day was Friday, we can only conclude that Jesus was brought before Pilate at about midnight—"the sixth hour"—on what we call Thursday night, but what, according to Genesis, chapter 1, and according to Jewish Sabbath-keeping, actually was Friday.

Accordingly, Jesus was arrested early Thursday morning; tried before Annas while it was yet dark (John 18:13); brought before Caiaphas in the assembly of the Sanhedrin (His legal trial) at daybreak (Matt. 26:57; 27:1); next before Pilate, Friday, before daybreak—about the sixth hour (John 19:14); then before Herod (Luke 23:7); then back to Pilate (Luke 23:11); and finally was crucified in the morning of the same day, about the third hour (Mark 15:25)—9:00 A.M., modern time.

This time-record shows that His capture,

His trials, and His crucifixion were carefully and cunningly prearranged to take place at night and early morning to prevent any uproar, for "they feared the people." Luke 20:19.

That He remained in the tomb two nights and rose on Sunday; that the three days and three nights is the time from His first legal trial to the time of His resurrection; that the heart of the earth has been erroneously interpreted to mean the grave, when, instead, it is, as Jonah's experience shows, symbolical of Christ's imprisonment in the hands of sinners and in the tomb (Matt. 20:19; 16:21; 17:22, 23; 27:63; Luke 9:22; 24:21; 18:33; 24:7;—"Thus it is written, and thus it behoved Christ to suffer, and to *rise* from the dead the third day." Luke 24:46); that the sign of the "three days and three nights" literally is fulfilled from Thursday morning, the time of His legal trial, to Sunday morning when He arose; that the paschal lamb, which was about to be killed when Jesus was on the cross, was not that which was killed on the first day of the Passover week, the fourteenth day of the month, but that which was killed on the sixteenth day, the second day of the feasts;—all these conclusions are firmly founded on the solid facts established herein in simplicity; not, dear reader, on fables or on translations unknown to you, or on so-called "original manuscripts," which you yourself cannot read, and which are not accessible to you, and some of which do not even exist!

Now to clear up other points in this connection, we shall consider the question:

Is the Evening the Beginning or the Ending of the Day?

Throughout the Bible, just as in books written in this age, the word "even" means the afternoon of the same day. Wednesday evening therefore means the ending of Wednesday and the beginning of Thursday, not the ending of Tuesday and the beginning of Wednesday, although Wednesday night coalesces with and becomes the night of Thursday. This fact will be readily seen from the following scriptures:

Early in the morning, "Mary Magdalene came and told the disciples that she had seen the Lord" (John 20:18); "then the same day at evening, being the first day of the week, . . . came Jesus and stood in the midst." John 20:19. Thus in Jesus's day, the term "evening" was used to designate the last part of the day.

Again: "And the first day of unleavened bread, when they killed the passover, His disciples said unto Him, Where wilt Thou that we go and prepare that Thou mayest eat the passover? And He sendeth forth two of His disciples, and saith unto them, Go ye into the city, and there shall meet you a man bearing a pitcher of water:

follow him . . . and he will shew you a large upper room furnished and prepared: there make ready for us . . . and in the evening He cometh with the twelve." Mark 14:12, 13, 15, 17.

Here Mark says that in the fourteenth day, when they killed the Passover lamb, Jesus sent forth two of His disciples, and that after they had prepared the place, and evening of that same day had come, then came Jesus. Thus in this scripture also, we see that the "evening" means, not the beginning, but the ending, of the day.

Again: "And it came to pass, that at even the quails came up." Ex. 16:13. As quails do not fly at night, they therefore had to come to the camp before sunset, the time which Moses calls "even"—the ending of the day, not the beginning of the night.

These Bible facts show that the Lord's command concerning the Passover lamb, "Ye shall keep it up until the fourteenth day . . . and . . . shall kill it in the evening" (Ex. 12:6), means that the lamb was to be killed in the afternoon of the fourteenth day. Consequently, to call Friday night "Sabbath *evening*," as some do, is unbiblical and unreliable, as is an

Opinion Based on Implication, a House Built on a Sandy Foundation.

The statement, "that same night He was taken by wicked hands, to be crucified and slain" (*The Great Controversy*, p. 399), does not mean, as some think, that He was crucified that night, but rather it means simply, just as it says, that He was "taken" *to be* crucified. Accordingly, though "taken that same night," He could have been crucified days after, if need be, and as actually was the case.

Likewise, neither does the statement, "On this last evening with His disciples" (*The Desire of Ages*, p. 643), mean that it was the last evening before He was crucified, but rather that it was the last evening *with His disciples* before His death.

The time-table in *The Shepherd's Rod*, Vol. 2, pp. 23-25, is not designed to show the precise time of the events as some, in their own interest, want to make it say; rather its purpose is only to give an idea of how long it *may* have taken to accomplish all that would have had to be done for the feast if the lamb had been killed just at the exact moment of the setting of the sun: showing the impossibility of accomplishing in one day all that was done in connection with the Passover, betrayal, trial, crucifixion, and burial.

Those who have attempted to crowd "the sixth hour" that signalized Jesus' trial in Pilate's judgment hall, and "the sixth hour" that commenced the darkness while He was on the cross, —a period of twelve hours,—into a "watch" of four hours, think the two scriptures are in perfect harmony with their idea, when, in plain fact, as here seen, they are as irreconcilable as night and day! Yet these same ones are having no end of perverse enjoyment in their not being able to reconcile the "midnight seizure" with the time as tabulated in the aforementioned time-table, which, according to their understanding, represents three or four hours discrepancy! Why have they not used the "watch system" here where it *can* be used?

The time-table is not endeavoring to show the "midnight seizure," but simply the time that the Jews "laid hold on Jesus"—when He was brought before the priests and, in particular, before the Sanhedrin (Matt. 26:57). (See chart, *The Shepherd's Rod*, Vol. 2, p. 22.) Whereas *The Desire of Ages*, pp. 699, 760, is speaking of the time that He was seized in the *garden* (Matt. 26:50)—the "midnight seizure."

If the midnight seizure, the trial before Pilate, the crucifixion, and the burial of Jesus, all took place in one day (Friday), then how could He have been seized in the garden *shortly after midnight*, led from there successively to Annas, to Caiaphas, to the Sanhedrin, and to Pilate, and yet be in Pilate's judgment hall *about midnight*? This utter impossibility alone should convince anyone with an understanding mind that these events must necessarily have consumed two days and that any argument supporting the idea that they consumed but one day, is not against the exposition of *The Shepherd's Rod*, but against the testimonies of Mark and John, who were eyewitnesses to these events.

Other such confusing remarks have been made, but as we have given due consideration to all the major ones, the minor ones merit no comment. Suffice it to say that our experience in gospel publishing work teaches us that many who have spent almost countless hours of precious time in confusing the subject of the sign of Jonah, have spent but very little time in studying more essential subjects such as the prohibition against private interpretations of the Scriptures (2 Pet. 1:19, 20); the Spirit of Prophecy (Rev. 19:10); the Sabbath (Ex. 20:8-11); baptism (Matt. 3:15; Acts 2:38); the Kingdom (Isa. 2:2); the slaughter of Ezekiel 9; tithe paying (Mal. 3:10); although these vital subjects call for performance,—a duty to practice the truths which they teach,—whereas the sign of Jonah demands nothing.

After one acquires all the knowledge necessary pertaining to the sign of Jonah, he is neither better nor worse off so far as his Christianity is concerned, without taking into account the time wasted if his conclusions on the subject be wrong.

But what is still worse, should a group of people who are rightly proclaiming all the revealed doctrines, disagree with these zealous preachers of the sign of Jonah, as to what "the heart of the earth" may mean, the latter will in most instances not only forsake fellowshiping with their brethren, and cease helping to proclaim the more important doctrines, but will also become so obsessed with their pet idea that their minds cannot comprehend much else.

To *just such a class of people* "He answered and said unto them, An evil and adulterous generation seeketh after a sign; and there shall no sign be given to it, but the sign of the prophet Jonas" (Matt. 12:39),—and here they have it!

The Jews actually saw the "sign," but because of their unbelief, they failed to profit by it. We hope, though, that the failure of the sign-seekers in those days will be a warning to the sign-seekers in these days.

Now, by studying the front-page chart, the reader can quickly summarize the entire subject, and thus obtain a lasting picture of the Scripturally immovable sign-posts of each event, concluding the impossibility of judging Him before *both* the Jewish and the Roman judiciaries, in addition to mocking and crucifying Him, in three short hours—from sunrise (the twelfth hour) to the third hour! In other words, the chart shows that it is utterly impossible in *three short hours* to have at least one trial before the Sanhedrin, two before Pilate, and one before Herod, making a total of no less than four trials, besides the time to crucify Him. Dividing the total time consumed (three hours) by the total number of events (five), we find that there would be only thirty-six minutes for each event! But merely walking from one place of judgment to another, along with arranging the trials, would alone have consumed more than three hours!

QUESTION AND ANSWER
DISCUSSION

DID JESUS EAT THE PASSOVER ON THE PASSOVER DAY?

Question:

Was Jesus supposed to have eaten the Passover on the first day of unleavened bread in the Passover week of the crucifixion, or beforehand?

Answer:

The time of the Passover observance being invoked by law, no one could celebrate its feast at another time and yet be rewarded as a Passover keeper. Much less, therefore, could Jesus have eaten it previously, because He would thereby not only have set a bad example but also have given the Jews occasion justly to accuse Him and to make much out of it, which, had it actually occurred, the apostles naturally would have recorded. The fact, though, that they did not make any such record, shows conclusively that there was none to make.

It was, moreover, on "the first day of unleavened bread," the day "they killed the passover" (not before), that "His disciples said unto Him, Where wilt Thou that we go and prepare that Thou mayest eat the Passover? . . . And in the evening He cometh with the twelve. And as they sat and did eat, Jesus said, Verily I say unto you, One of you which eateth with Me shall betray Me." Mark 14:12, 17, 18.

Here the Bible states in as clear language as possible that Jesus with the twelve ate the Passover at the time set by the Mosaic law.

DID JESUS EAT THE PASSOVER THE DAY OF HIS CRUCIFIXION?

Question:

The Desire of Ages, p. 642, says: " . . . on the day the Passover was eaten, Christ was to be sacrificed." If the Passover was eaten Wednesday night, how could He have been crucified on Friday, and yet the statement be true?

Answer:

If the questioner will carefully read the entire context of the statement in question, he will quickly see that he is misinterpreting the word "sacrificed" as used by the author. The author herself interprets it to

—23—

mean His "suffering," a term which cannot be limited to His crucifixion, but which includes, as the context of the statement in question shows, His trials, abuse, and crucifixion:

"In the upper chamber of a dwelling at Jerusalem, Christ was sitting at table with His disciples. They had gathered to celebrate the Passover. The Saviour desired to keep this feast alone with the twelve. He knew that His hour was come; He Himself was the true paschal lamb, and on the day the Passover was eaten, He was to be sacrificed. He was about to drink the cup of wrath; He must soon receive the final baptism of *suffering*. But a few quiet hours yet remained to Him, and these were to be spent for the benefit of His beloved disciples."—*The Desire of Ages*, p. 642.

ON WHAT DAY WAS THE PASSOVER?

Question:

How can one determine the day of the week upon which fell the fourteenth day of the first month (the beginning of the Passover week in which Christ was crucified)? How can one prove that it was Wednesday?

Answer:

As a period of three days and three nights was consumed in trying, mocking, scourging, and, finally, in crucifying Christ, and then in His dying, being in the tomb, and rising (see Matthew 20:19; 16:21; 17:22, 23; 27:63; Luke 9:22; 24:21; 18:33; 24:7, 46), then counting backwards three days and three nights from Sunday, the day He arose (Mark 16:9), gives Wednesday. Thus it was Wednesday night in which He ate the Passover supper with the twelve.

CAN ONE DAY HAVE TWO MORNINGS?

Question:

In speaking of Judas at the trial before Caiaphas, *The Desire of Ages*, p. 722, says: "Eagerly grasping the robe of Caiaphas, he implored him to release Jesus . . . *Later that same day*, on the road from Pilate's hall to Calvary, there came an interruption to the shouts and jeers of the wicked throng who were leading Jesus to the place of crucifixion."

Here *The Desire of Ages* says that both the trial before Caiaphas and the trial before Pilate, also the crucifixion, took place in the same day, whereas *The Shepherd's Rod* clearly proves from the Bible that the trials and the crucifixion took two days.

How, then, can *The Desire of Ages* be reconciled to the Bible?

Answer:

Bear in mind the fact that Christ was tried seven times in all: "twice before the priests, twice before the Sanhedrin, twice before Pilate, and once before Herod" (*The Desire of Ages*, p. 760). The first two were before day break (John 18:13, 24), and the third began with day break (Matt. 26:57; 27:1).

Now according to the time of the day, the trial before Pilate came earlier (while it was dark—John 18:28, 29; John 19:14) than the one before the Sanhedrin (at day break), but chronologically (actually) the one before the Sanhedrin came first, and the one before Pilate afterwards. These two trials, therefore, could not have occurred the same day.

Hence the statement, "that same day," cannot refer to the day Jesus was arrested, but to a day later, as *The Desire of Ages* itself makes clear:

"*As soon as it was day*, the Sanhedrin again assembled, and again Jesus was brought into the council room." —*The Desire of Ages*, p. 714.

"The Roman governor had been called from his bedchamber in haste, and he determined to do his work as quickly as possible. . . . he turned to see what kind of man he had to examine, that he had been called from his repose at *so early an hour*." —*The Desire of Ages,* p. 723.

From these citations it is seen that *The Desire of Ages* recognizes that the events were on two different mornings: the one before Caiaphas, "as soon as it was day," and the other before Pilate, also "at so early an hour."

Then, too, the fact that "hour after hour went by" before the Sanhedrin "trial drew to a close" (*Id.* p. 721), shows that it went on late into the day.

The Desire of Ages, p. 722, is dealing with the entire judicial proceedings, not in its seven component scenes, but as a composite whole—one sustained trial. For Judas became desperate after having seen that Jesus was in every trial condemned to be crucified, and so he went out and hanged himself.

Hence *The Desire of Ages* is in perfect harmony with the Bible, but the questioner has failed to read between the lines.

A PASSOVER FEAST THEORY ATTEMPTING TO SUPPORT LUNAR SABBATH KEEPING

Question:

In an effort to build up its private theory, a brochure entitled *The Sabbath of Creation* contends that the Passover feast was observed in the beginning of the fourteenth day of the first month, fixing the thirteenth day of the same month as the preparation to kill the Passover lamb. Is this correct?

Answer:

"In the fourteenth day of the first month at even is the Lord's Passover. And *on the fifteenth* day of the same month is the feast of unleavened bread." Lev. 23:5, 6.

Plainly, therefore, they were to kill the Passover lamb in the afternoon of the fourteenth day, and were to have the feast in the night or at the beginning of the fifteenth day.

The booklet also contends that Jesus died on the thirteenth day of the month, which, according to its calculations, happened just about when the Passover lamb of the fourteenth day was to be killed. Whereas Matthew, Mark, Luke, and John—all four of the gospels—agree that "the first day of unleavened bread, when they killed the passover, His disciples said unto Him, Where wilt Thou that we go and prepare that Thou mayest eat the Passover?" Having prepared the same, "they sat and did eat." Mark 14:12, 18; Matt. 26:1-21; Luke 22:1-15; John 13:1, 2.

Assuming that the seventh-day Sabbath is governed by the lunar calendar, instead of by the independent weekly cycle,

The Brochure Says:

"Yes, all Christendom, with the exception of some Saturday keepers, keep a heathen day of the Sun. But the Saturday keepers also keep, and honor a day of

—28—

heathen origin—the day of Saturn. All these days, with their system of nomenclature came to the Greeks and Romans, thence to all the world from Egypt, where Julius Caesar got his calendar of 365 days to the year, but added one-fourth day to it every year. Both are false.

"The Egyptians' first day of their week was Saturn's day (Saturday) and moonday (Monday) their seventh day. They had seven days to their week. But the Romans, at this time and to the time of Constantine, had eight days to their week. (See New International Encyclopedia, Vol. 23, p. 436, for proof.) So, the Saturday, like the Sunday, is of heathen, human, origin, and not of God. But when the Romans officially adopted the seven-day week from Egypt (where Julius had also gotten his 365 days to the year, though adding an extra one-fourth day to each year), from the days of Constantine, 321 A.D. to the days of Theodosius the Great, about 75 years later, the Romans reversed the nomenclature of the Egyptians by making Sunday (the mid-week day of Egypt) to head the week of their own calendar. Thus the day of the Sun was made to head the week, as Julius Caesar had made January (from Janus, Sun-god) to be the father of the year. And Saturday was made the Seventh Day of the week of their calendar, and this calendar was later enforced by the Catholic church of that same power upon the whole world, and observed by all

Christendom till this day. It is this fact that has called forth from God the Third Angel's Message to call out His people from this service to Rome under the penalty of suffering the seven last plagues unless they turn from the Roman service to His, in Sabbath keeping. . . .

"Exodus 12:1, 2: 'And the Lord spake unto Moses and Aaron in the land of Egypt, saying, This month shall be unto you the beginning of months: it shall be the first month (moon) of the year to you.' The moon was made to measure the months. Compare 1 Samuel 20, verses 5, 18, 24, 27, 34. And also to mark the seasons (Gen. 1:14 and Psa. 104:19). The moon and the sun and the stars is God's calendar in the firmament that all men can see and mark God's times together with the earth. . . .

"The Sabbath of the Bible, therefore, is the Sabbath upon which the Passover comes every year. The Lord has purposely placed the Passover celebration upon the second Sabbath of the first Moon (Abib), every year, for a reminder of the Sabbath every year (Ex. 20:8). It is the second Sabbath of the first month, by reason of the Passover being upon the fourteenth of that month, which is the first full moon after the Vernal equinox when spring begins."—The Sabbath of Creation, pp. 9, 10, 13, 14, 16.

To the exponents of such Sabbath reckoning as aforequoted, the Spirit of Truth gives

The Reply:

In the italicized paragraphs, the well-intentioned but grossly misinformed author is attempting to overthrow the present weekly seventh-day Sabbath by attacking the independent weekly cycle and by favoring the lunar calendar. He sets forth the seventh, the fourteenth, the twenty-first, and the twenty-eighth days of each lunar cycle as commemorative sabbaths of the week of creation.

We do not dispute that the early Romans had such an eight-day week, and that the names of the months and days of the week are of mythological derivation, but we do ask the lunar-sabbath author for evidence based on facts, not on assumption, that the Sabbath of creation was ever governed by the lunar cycle. True, the Lord said to Moses, "This month shall be unto you the beginning of months: it shall be the first month of the year to you." Ex. 12:2. But He did not say, "It is the beginning of your *weeks*." Indeed He could not have, for such a course would be

Contrary to Nature and to Logic.

If any one of the two luminary planets should be honored to govern the holy Sabbath, it should be the sun, the one which rules not only the moon but also the entire system. Had God intended the moon to be the time regulator and indicator, the system would have been entitled *lunar* instead of *solar*. Had He, moreover, intended the moon to fix the time of the holy Sabbath, He would have made it to complete its revolution round the earth, if not once in exactly 4 weeks, then once in exactly a whole week, or in exactly a day. And had He, furthermore, intended for the sun to point out the holy time, the earth must, then, have completed her revolution round it in exactly 52 weeks.

We shall now briefly bring forth existing solar, lunar, and Biblical facts, not implications, that the weekly cycle cannot be and has never been controlled by any monthly calendar; that neither the Old nor the New Testament church under God's direction has at any time kept a lunar seventh-day sabbath; that the booklet, *The Sabbath of Creation*, is falsely so-entitled; and that

The Weekly Cycle Is Neither Solar Nor
Lunar.

The Sabbath on which the Lord rested was exactly six days after the moment creation began; then, on the seventh day He rested (Gen. 2:2). Had He, though, blessed a day which is ruled by the moon, He would have then rested the tenth day, for the moon was not created until the fourth day of creation. (See Genesis 1:14-19.) But keeping a Sabbath on the seventh day from the creation of the moon, would not have been in commemoration of creation, but in commemoration of the moon!

The first Sabbatical week of creation's being three days older than both the sun and the moon, makes it clear that neither of the luminaries can regulate the week of creation. Such a regulatory force would of necessity have deprived Time and Creation of the first three days, leaving them as a phantom "lost period."

The two foregoing paragraphs completely invalidate the idea of the week's being dependent upon the monthly orbit of the moon, and render unnecessary any further discussion of the subject. For the sake, however, of clearing some other controverted points, as well as for saving ourselves time later on in answering detailed questions on this subject, we submit the subjoined observations. From them the reader is asked to consider that if a lunar sabbath were correctly named, should it not be named, not the sabbath of creation, but rather

Only a Planetary Sabbath?

The Lord having rested on the "seventh day," not on the tenth, the weekly cycle began with the first day of creation, whereas solar and lunar time commenced three days later. A sabbath which is governed by either a solar or a lunar calendar, though, could never memorialize the week of creation, but rather only the planets themselves, and therefore, if correctly named, must be called "planetary." Then, too, the monthly revolution of the moon round the earth, not coordinating with the daily revolution of the earth round the sun, as already pointed out, makes it

Impossible to Keep a Planetary Sabbath.

The fact that the moon takes longer than 28 days to complete its revolution round the earth, then were we to standardize the seventh, the fourteenth, the twenty-first, and the twenty-eighth days of the lunar month, for the observance of the Sabbath, as the misnamed booklet advocates, we would not have kept up with the moon anyway, for the lunar month is not actually 28 days, but approximately 29-1/2 days.

A lunar sabbath must necessarily coordinate with both lunar and solar time. But a sabbatical month (28 days) falls 1 ½ days short of a lunar month (29 ½); and a sabbatical year (12 x 4 = 48 weeks; 48 x 7 = 336 days) falls 18 days short of a lunar year (354) and 29 days short of a solar year (365). So at the close of each sabbatical year, the lunar sabbath-keeper, in order to keep time with the weekly cycle, as well as with the rotation of the earth and of the moon, would have to make the earth stand still 29 days and the moon 18 days.

This analysis corroborates the fact that the weekly cycle cannot be governed by the motion of either the moon or the sun, but only by the power of God, which brought forth the first day of creation, three days before there was either sun or moon. And so, as we are again shown, the Sabbath is a memorial, not of the sun or the moon, but of creation.

There is no doubt in the minds of any that the Jewish and Apostolic churches in Christ's time were keeping the right Sabbath day; and that the zeal which the Roman Emperor, Constantine, had for the Christian faith would have absolutely forbidden him to abolish the Christian's calendar and to establish another which would annihilate both the Sabbath of creation and their memorial of the resurrection.

Surely no one supposes that had he done such an impious thing, the Christians would have honored him so greatly as to call him a saint and to fix the twentieth day of May as his festival, which some observe even until this day. (See *Twentieth Century Cyclopaedia*, Vol. 3, p. 13)

Indeed, the Christians would have made so much of his sacrilege that no conceivable circumstance could have concealed the blasphemous act from the prying eye of history. But such an entry is not to be found in

"The use of the week was introduced into the Roman Empire about the 1st or 2nd century of the Christian era from Egypt and had been recognized independently of Christianity before the Emperor Constantine confirmed it by enjoining the observance of the Christian Sabbath. With the Mohammedans the week has also a religious character, Friday being observed by them as a Sabbath."—*Twentieth Century Cyclopaedia*, Vol. 8, p. 487.

"The period of seven days . . . was used by the Brahmins in India with the same denominations employed by us, and *was alike found in* the calendars of the Jews, Egyptians, Arabs and Assyrians."—*Standard Dictionary*, definition "Calendar."

"The week is a period of seven days having no reference whatever to the celestial motions,—a circumstance to which it owes its unalterable uniformity. It was employed from time immemorial in almost all eastern countries; and, as it forms neither an aliquot part of the year nor of the lunar month, those who reject the Mosaic recital will be at a loss, as Dalambre remarks, to assign it to an origin having such semblance of possibility."—*Britannica Encyclopedia*.

"It is our pleasure (such is the Imperial style) that all the nations, which are governed by our clemency and moderation, should steadfastly adhere to the religion which was taught by St. Peter to the Romans; which faithful tradition has preserved; and which is now professed by the Pontiff Damasus, and by Peter, Bishop of Alexandria, a man of Apostolic holiness. According to the discipline of the Apostles, and the doctrine of the Gospel, let us believe the sole deity of the Father, the Son, and the Holy Ghost; under an equal majesty, and a pious Trinity. We authorize the followers of this doctrine to assume the title of Catholic Christians; and as we judge, that all others are extravagant madmen, we brand them with the infamous name of Heretics; and declare that their conventicles shall no longer usurp the respectable appellation of churches."—*Gibbon's Rome*, Vol. 3, p. 81. (Milman edition.)

This historical record plainly shows that the weekly period of seven days has continued unbroken from time immemorial, that Rome did not abolish the Christian week but the Roman, and that the one which took its place was the same as the Jewish, or the Christian.

Even the lunar-sabbath advocate, himself, unwittingly admits that Constantine, in the days of his conversion to Christianity, discarded the eight-day week and adopted and confirmed the seven-day week—the week of creation: "*These three witnesses* [*The New International Encyclope-*

dia, Encyclopedia Britannica, and Encyclopedia Americana]," says the brochure, "*tell us that the Romans did not have seven days to their week, nor their astrological names, till the days of Constantine, but that up to that time they had eight days.*"—*The Sabbath of Creation,* p. 24.

Though the nations of today do not follow the Biblical monthly calendar, that in no wise alters the fact that the original weekly cycle has never been changed. And as it is entirely independent of both the solar and the lunar calendars, had God not preserved it intact throughout all the ages, the saints, now in "the times of restitution of all things," would have great difficulty to restore it and to vindicate its integrity. Thus it is seen from every test put to it, that such a lunar sabbath is unbiblical and unhistorical; and the closer it is brought to the light, the plainer it will be seen to be

Even More Illogical.

It is true that the ceremonial system (younger than the Sabbath institution, and set up because sin entered into the human family) was in some respects subject to lunar laws; but the seventh-day Sabbath's being established, *not* in relation to sin, but only in relation to the perfect work of creation, could no more be governed by the law of sin than it could by the law of the moon. The Sabbath institution is senior to the ceremonial institution and has nothing to do with the law of sin, as has the Sanctuary. The Sabbath, therefore, cannot bow down in subservience to an institution which is not only its junior but which also owes its existence solely to sin!

Again we see that this author's theory of a "Planetary Sabbath" is blasphemous as well as unreasonable and futile.

The theorist has used the writings of certain historians, but let the student of Truth closely examine the quotations, and he will find that they do not support the theory any more than the Bible supports it, which leads to

The Theorist's Main Trouble.

Going off on such tangents is due to shallow reading and to interpreting the words of others without digging deep enough to find the thought of the original authors. And the main reason that advocates of error stay in their errors is that most of them are determined at any cost to stand by their self-made theories! And that is their main trouble. But we hope and pray that these mistaken brethren will welcome the Truth as contained in the plain, pointed, unglossed, and fundamental facts set forth in these pages, and allow It to lodge in their hearts. Thus only may they be led to walk in the light and to find rest in Him Who is anxious to lead us into all Truth, and Who, therefore, sends this

Watch your steps, and pay no homage to either a moon or a sun sabbath-day. For by sacredly honoring such a common day, you would be worshiping those things which were created in the last three days of creation's week; namely, the planets of the heavens and the creatures of the sea, the fowls of the air and the creeping things of the ground, the beasts of the field and the mortal man of clay!

Follow the leadership of God instead of the leadership of the moon. Be ye not idolators, for " . . . it shall come to pass in that day, saith the Lord of hosts, that I will cut off the names of the idols out of the land, and they shall no more be remembered: and also I will cause the prophets and the unclean spirit to pass out of the land." Zech. 13:2.

A FLOOD OF RELIGIOUS LITERATURE

Question:

A flood of religious literature varied and contradictory is coming to me, and I do not know what to make of it all, as one piece is endeavoring to indoctrinate me in one way, and another piece in the opposite way, and still other pieces in still other ways, with the result that should I try at the same time to go all the ways advocated or commanded, I would, so to speak, be running around myself. What hope is there to find one's way through such a maze of doctrines? On one hand, I fear that if I study into it all, it may cause me to lose sight even of the truth which I now have; and on the other hand, I fear that if I do not study it, I may turn down some precious present truth, and thus lose eternity.

The very fact that there are so many winds of doctrine blowing is, to my mind, manifest evidence that the Lord must have a message in the land, and that the great flood of religious literature overflowing the religious world is being poured out in the desperate attempt to drown out the voice of the Lord's message for today.

So as you seem to have better Bible grounds for your positions than the others do for theirs, and as you also have singular Scriptural endorsement (Mic. 6:9) for hearing your message, I am taking courage to turn to you in the hope that the voice of the Rod will lead me out of the confusion of voices that are crying "lo here" and "lo there."

First will you help me to test the British Israel theory concerning the kingdom?

Answer:

The questioner is obviously correct as to the reason for the many winds of doctrine blowing today. And in view of this confusion of voices, his fears concerning listening to them are understandable, and makes the more commendable his determination to discharge his God-imposed responsibility of personal investigation:

"Thus saith the Lord, *Stand ye in the ways*, and see, and ask for the old paths, where is the good way, and walk therein, and ye shall find rest for your souls. But they said, We will not walk therein." Jer. 6:16. "Beloved, believe not every spirit, but *try the spirits* whether they are of God: because many false prophets are gone out into the world." 1 John 4:1.

To relegate everything to the waste basket certainly is not only to cast out the very truth, but also to disregard the Lord's command as seen in the verses already quoted.

For every truth-seeker, moreover, stands the promise that He will not let one of them be deceived: "God never honors unbelief and questioning and doubt. When He speaks, His word is to be recognized and carried out in the daily actions. And if the heart of man is in living connection with God, the voice that cometh from above *will be recognized*. . . . Those that do the will of God *shall know* of the doctrine whether it be of God, for *no deception* will cloud their minds."—*Testimonies on Sabbath-School Work*, pp. 64, 65.

With these sure promises to stand upon, let us now examine

The British-Israel Doctrine.

A periodical entitled, *Kingdom Correspondence School*, states the movement's position: "*We Anglo-Saxons are the same people who existed under the name of Israel in the Old Testament day. . . .*

" *. . . The Kings from Solomon, in a direct, unbroken line extends to the present King—George VI—on the throne in England today. We believe that the Lord—who is the King of kings of the tribe of Judah and of the House of David—for He is the Lion of the tribe of Judah, (Rev. 5:5) and that He will soon return and take over the throne of His father, David.*" pp. 1, 8.

The author of this statement contends that though God's ancient people submerged as the kingdom of Israel, they have emerged today as the kingdom of Great Britain. But speaking of the Israelitish Kingdom and its people, the Spirit of Prophecy, in ancient time, said:

"Moreover I will make thee waste, and a reproach among the nations that are round about thee, in the sight of all that pass by." "A third part of thee shall die with the pestilence, and with famine shall they be consumed in the midst of thee: and a third part shall fall by the sword round about thee; and I will scatter a third part into all the winds, and I will draw out a sword after them. Thus shall Mine anger be accomplished, and I will cause My fury to rest upon them, and I will be comforted: and they shall know that I the Lord have spoken it in My zeal, when I have accomplished My fury in them. Moreover I will make thee waste, and a reproach among the nations that are round about thee, in the sight of all that pass by. . . . "Therefore thus saith the Lord God; Behold, I, even I, am against thee, and will execute judgments in the midst of thee in the sight of the nations. And I will do in thee that which I have not done, and whereunto I will not do any more the like, because of all thine abominations. . . . " "I will overturn, overturn, overturn, it: and it shall be no more, until He come Whose right it is; and I will give it Him." Ezek. 5:12-14, 8, 9; 21:27.

"For the head of Syria is Damascus, and the head of Damascus is Rezin; and within threescore and five years shall Ephraim be broken, that it be not a people." Isa. 7:8.

The aforementioned periodical especially emphasizes that England is the tribe of Ephraim, although the sure word of prophecy categorically states that Ephraim shall "be not a people." Thus the prophecies declare that the Israelitish kingdom was to cease, and that the people were to be driven among the nations of the earth. Nevertheless, there is a promise that after years of dispersion, the Lord "will take the children of Israel from among the heathen, whither they be gone, and will gather them on every side, and bring them into their own land." Ezek. 37:21.

"And He shall set up an ensign for the nations, and shall assemble the outcasts of Israel, and gather together the dispersed of Judah from the four corners of the earth." Isa. 11:12.

"For the children of Israel shall abide many days without a king, and without a prince, and without a sacrifice, and without an image, and without an ephod, and without teraphim: afterward shall the children of Israel return, and seek the Lord their God, and David their king; and shall fear the Lord and His goodness in the latter days." Hosea 3:4, 5. "And the Gentiles shall see thy righteousness, and all kings thy glory: and thou shalt be called by a new name, which the mouth of the Lord shall name. Thou shalt also be a crown of glory in the hand of the Lord, and a royal diadem in the hand of thy God. Thou shalt no more be termed Forsaken; neither shall thy land any more be termed Desolate: but thou shalt be called Hephzibah, and thy land Beulah: for the Lord delighteth in thee, and thy land shall be married. And they shall call them, The holy people, The redeemed of the Lord: and thou shalt be called, Sought out, A city not forsaken." Isa. 62:2-4, 12.

These scriptures plainly set forth the fact that God was to scatter Israel throughout the nations, leave them without a king or a home-land for "many days," and finally gather them one by one from every nation. At that time shall they choose David their king, and be "the holy people." Isa. 62:12.

For detailed treatment of the Kingdom, read our tracts No. 8, *Mount Sion at the Eleventh Hour*, and No. 12, *The World, Yesterday, Today, and Tomorrow*.

The questions herein treated reveal that an unseen supernatural force working through human beings, is taking advantage of every possible opportunity to bring in distraction and confusion and to scatter the power of thought and concentration. They show that while one theorist is attempting to confuse one truth, another theorist is attempting to confuse another truth. So it is obvious that the enemy of God and men is determined one way or another to plunge the people into his deep pit. To avert this terrible tragedy, the reader is therefore warned to turn aside from the writings of uninspired men, and to take heed only to those who are inspired, and unceasingly to watch and study everything that comes in the name of the Lord.

(All italics ours)

For further study on the subject of the sign of Jonah, read Vol. 2 of *The Shep-*

herd's Rod, pp. 17-26; *The Symbolic Code*, Vol. 1, No. 6, pp. 5-7 (1934); Vol. 2, No. 12, p. 6 (1936); Vol. 3, Nos. 8-9-10, p. 10 (1937).

———————

Anyone sending us names and addresses of seventh-day Sabbath-keepers, will be entitled to receive, free of charge, our entire Present Truth series of thirteen tracts to date, and our official organ, *The Symbolic Code* (in which all readers' questions are answered).

SPIRIT OF PROPHECY INDEX

SCRIPTURAL INDEX

www.ingramcontent.com/pod-product-compliance
Lightning Source LLC
Chambersburg PA
CBHW061720120626
46550CB00003B/1302